LIGHT FR(

THE SEVEN LAST WORDS OF JESUS

Robert H. Ireland

O send out thy light and thy truth.—Psalm 43:3

THE BANNER OF TRUTH TRUST

THE BANNER OF TRUTH TRUST

Head Office
3 Murrayfield Road
Edinburgh, EH12 6EL
UK

North America Office
610 Alexander Spring Road
Carlisle, PA 17015
USA

banneroftruth.org

First published by James Nisbet & Co., London, 1873
This edition © The Banner of Truth Trust, 2024

*

ISBN
Print: 978 1 80040 430 4
Epub: 978 1 80040 431 1

*

Typeset in 11/14 Adobe Garamond Pro at
The Banner of Truth Trust, Edinburgh

Printed in the USA by
Versa Press Inc.,
East Peoria, IL

Contents

Preface

SEVEN words of Jesus spoken on his cross! You catch the last words of any dying man! You pause with interest at the record, 'These be the last words of David!' He that hath an ear, let him hear the voice of the dying Lord!

Beautifully have these seven words been called 'The bright lights of heaven shining at intervals through the darkness,' 'The deep solemn tones which interpret the cross,' 'The blossoms of the green tree which is in the flames, burning, not consumed.'

Seven words! The sacred seven-number of Scripture, denoting completeness. It is the full gospel of salvation from the lips of the dying Saviour. Verily, O Jesus, 'grace is poured into thy lips,' and to all eternity we shall 'wonder at the gracious words which proceeded out of thy mouth,' when hanging as a curse for us on the tree of Calvary!

O Christ of God! Prophet, Priest, and King! Speak to our hearts from thy throne now, through these voices from thy cross!

'O send out thy light and thy truth.'

I

Father, forgive them; for they know not what they do.

He looks and calls from high,
   Art thou to die or live?
He hears the posts and lintels cry,
   Forgive, forgive, forgive!

I

Father, forgive them; for they know not what they do.—
LUKE 23:34

CALVARY is reached. The soldiers begin the cruel work. They nail the blessed Jesus to a cross between two thieves—'on either side one, and Jesus in the midst.' The *blood* drops from his pierced hands and feet, and the *word* drops from his lips, 'Father, forgive them; for they know not what they do.'

The soldiers hear it. The thieves on the cross hear it. The people that 'stand beholding' hear it. The Father in heaven hears it—'Father, forgive them.'

I think first of the love of Jesus, the perfect love of the holy Jesus, living on even unto death. Love reigns still, as ever, in that great heart—'Father, forgive them.' I think next of the quick utterance of the plea for pardon the moment that atoning blood is shed, as if to say, The way is open now, every barrier removed, the deep channel dug for the outflow of Heaven's pardoning love—'Father, forgive them.'

I cannot but turn to the immediate crucifiers of Jesus, to the four soldiers whose hands did the work; and as perhaps they were but instruments in other hands, which had the greater sin, there may have been the loving thought and pleading prayer for them, 'They know not what they do.' But the prayer extends beyond these, far beyond, not only to all the others who had any part, direct or indirect, in the crucifixion, but to all in every age, to sinners everywhere whose sins nailed the Son of God to Calvary's cross, whose sins he 'bare in his own body on the tree.' Thank God, that down the stream of time the blessing of forgiveness comes, which was asked of the Father the first moment that the blood of atonement was shed; for the voice of Jesus asked articulately what the blood itself asked, and asks still while days of mercy last—'Father, forgive them.'

I. I point to *sin*—sin as needing forgiveness.

I take the deep tone of meaning to be—'they know not *what* they do.' They have no idea of the tremendous sin they are committing, they have no idea of the wisdom of God, the hidden wisdom; for 'had they known they would not have crucified the Lord of glory' (1 Cor. 2:8). I think that, viewing these soldiers who crucified our Lord as but the type of sinners everywhere, and the prayer of Jesus as offered for all for whom he died, the word tells of the magnitude of the sin, a sin the magnitude of which men only come to know when pardoning love reaches their hearts, a sin which many of the very people who crucified Jesus came to know when, under the preaching of the gospel, 'with the Holy Ghost sent down from heaven,' the light shone in, and the truth flashed on their souls—'We have crucified the Lord of glory'; and the cry came up from the depths of their stricken hearts, 'What shall we do?' We now know what we have done, what shall we do, not to undo it, for that cannot be, but what shall we do to be saved?

Strange scene at Calvary! None know in all its import what is done, save the man upon the cross himself, and the Father in heaven to whom he prays!

Strange scene now! A world of gospel-despisers, and none knowing the depth of guilt but the Saviour, the God whom men reject; but looking from his cross on the miserable condition of men as sinners, and drawing a reason from it, urging it as a plea for mercy and pity and pardon, Jesus says—'Father, forgive them; for they know not what they do.'

II. I point to *forgiveness*—God's forgiveness. If this word of the dying Saviour tells of *sin*, if it speaks of sin as God knows it, and as man knows it not, at least until he is either saved on earth or lost in hell, it only tells of it that it may tell of *forgiveness*, forgiveness for sinners now, forgiveness through the blood of Jesus, forgiveness prayed for by the dying high priest, as his first word on his very cross.

What is forgiveness? It is the discharge from the guilt of sin, it is the cancelling of the obligation to punishment. But sin cannot be forgiven without satisfaction rendered to the justice of God, and so, there is blood shed for the remission of sins, and the blood of God's own Son, our surety, is the meritorious cause of God's forgiveness. 'God for Christ's sake hath forgiven you' (Eph. 4:32). 'He hath made us accepted in the beloved, in whom we have redemption through his blood, the forgiveness of sins, according to the riches of his grace' (Eph. 1:6, 7). This is now the word of the gospel, that 'through this man is preached unto us the forgiveness of sins' (Acts 13:38), for 'him hath God exalted with his right hand to be a Prince and a Saviour, for to give repentance to Israel, and forgiveness of sins' (Acts 5:31).

Forgiveness of sins! We know not its value until sin is felt, until we come, through grace, in some degree to realise what it is to have the guilt of sin lying on our head, and pressing on our conscience, what it is to feel bound over by the righteous law of God to everlasting punishment, what it is to feel the justice of the sentence, and the keenness of anticipated suffering, because it is sin against one so loving while so holy. It is then that the name of forgiveness is so blessed; it is then that the cry for pardon is so long and loud; it is then that the blessing is experienced by the weeping sinner at the feet of Jesus.

Fellow sinner, are you forgiven? In your case, is the bond cancelled, is the obligation discharged, are you free? O happy soul, if you are! And if you are, you have known something of the Holy Spirit's work, who first teaches a man to feel his sin, and then leads him to the Saviour; who first takes of the things of Jesus and his cross, and shows a man his guilt, and then takes of these same things, yea of the very blood of Jesus, and speaks to that sin-burdened soul pardon and peace.

So was it when this prayer of Jesus first was answered. I know not what sense of sin the centurion may have had, when he 'saw what was done, and glorified God, saying, Certainly this was a righteous man.' I know not how these soldiers felt, if they felt their sin at all, of whom we read, 'Now, when the centurion, and they that were with him watching Jesus, saw the earthquake, and those things that were done, they feared greatly, saying, Truly this was the Son of God.' I know not what was in the hearts of those who came together, hardened enough, to that sight, but 'beholding the things which were done, smote upon their breasts and returned.' But I know something of the feelings of that dying thief who rebuked his fellow with the word, 'We indeed justly, for we receive the due reward of our deeds,' and who cried to the Saviour at his side, 'Lord, remember me when thou comest into thy kingdom.' I know something of the feelings of these three thousand on the day of Pentecost, who listened to Peter's preaching of sin first, and forgiveness next. I know that these men were made to know what they had done. It was the first lesson Peter gave them, and the first lesson the Holy Spirit taught them: 'Him ye have taken, and by wicked hands have crucified and slain. Therefore let all the house of Israel know assuredly, that God hath made that same Jesus, whom ye have crucified, both Lord and Christ. Now when they heard this, they were pricked in their heart, and said unto Peter, and to the rest of the apostles, Men and brethren, what shall we do?' (Acts 2:36, 37). Ah! now they know what they have done, and the question is, what are they to do next? And then it is that forgiveness is preached through the man Christ Jesus, and in the way in which alone a sinner can know its value—'Repent, and be baptized, every one of you, in the name of Jesus Christ, for the remission of sins.'

This is forgiveness, as man needs it and as God gives it. It is the same for us as for those to whom Peter preached, for he adds, 'The promise is unto you, and to your children, and to all that are afar off, even as many as the Lord our God shall call.'

III. Listen now to the *Great Intercessor's Prayer*.

'He was numbered with the transgressors, and he bare the sin of many, and made intercession for the transgressors' (Isa. 53:12), and lo! here is his word for the transgressors, as he is nailed to the cross to bear their sins, 'Father, forgive them.' What love! what amazing love! what a heart must Jesus have, aye, and what a heart must the Father have, whom he knows so well as to ask from him forgiveness at such an hour and for such sinners! Can our hearts conceive it! Can the tongue of man tell it? We can only listen and wonder, and pray that it may melt our hearts, and the hearts of thousands more, to hear that prayer.

Blessed connection between forgiveness and atonement! We see the blood, and we hear the cry, 'Forgive,'—it is blood shed for the remission of sins—aye, and in that blood there is complete satisfaction rendered to all the demands of the holy law, to all the claims of justice, so that it is not only mercy's voice we hear, but the voice of eternal justice too, crying 'Forgive, Forgive.' Oh! how blessed it is to see that divine grace and mercy rest on such a foundation as this; how blessed to know that when I, a poor sinner, seek forgiveness now, I seek it not, as in vain it would be sought, at the sacrifice of justice, but in the very exercise of justice. Mercy long held back the hand of justice, crying, 'Spare, spare the sinner, until the victim shall die on Calvary's cross'; and when he died, then the voice of the blood, and the voice of the Saviour, the voice of justice, and the voice of mercy, all cried to heaven, 'Forgive, forgive.'

Have we not, too, the connection here between the two great parts of our high priest's work, atonement and intercession? The atoning blood is shed, and the interceding voice is heard; the very moment that that blood is shed the voice is raised, as if Heaven's work were begun already, the first note of the prayer for sinners, as in the seventeenth chapter of John you have the first note of the prayer for saints.

If we view the first word from the cross in its *primary reference* to the immediate murderers of Jesus, what encouragement it affords to us, and all who feel themselves to be sinners, even the chief! It is as if our loving Saviour stooped to the lowest depths, as if on very purpose he singled out those who had even literally imbrued their hands in his blood, just to show us his heart, just to show us that his salvation is for the very chief of sinners. Akin to this is the word of our Lord, 'Thus it is written, and thus it behoved Christ to suffer, and to rise from the dead the third day, and that repentance and remission of sins should be preached in his name among all nations, beginning at Jerusalem' (Luke 24:46, 47).

Two hundred years ago an old divine preached from the text 'Beginning at Jerusalem,' one of the most touching and powerful sermons, I believe, ever penned. The Saviour is introduced as giving the apostles direction how to proceed in carrying out their great commission. Among other things he is represented as saying, 'Go unto all nations, and offer this salvation as you go; but, lest the poor house of Israel should think themselves abandoned to despair, the seed of Abraham, mine ancient friend, as cruel and unkind as they have been, go make *them* the first offer of grace; let them that struck the rock drink first of its refreshing stream, and they that drew my blood be welcome to its healing virtue. Tell them that, as I was sent to the lost sheep of the house of Israel, so if they will be gathered, I will be their shepherd still. Though they despised my tears which I shed over them, and imprecated my blood to be upon them, tell them 'twas for their sakes I shed both. Tell them you have seen the prints of the nails upon my hands and feet, and the wound of the spear in my side, and that those marks of their cruelty are so far from giving me vindictive thoughts, that if they will but repent, every wound they have given me speaks in their behalf, pleads with the Father for the remission of their sins, and enables me to bestow it. Nay, if you meet that poor wretch that thrust the spear into my side, tell him there is another way, a better way, of coming at my heart; if he will repent, and look upon him whom he has pierced, and mourn, I will cherish him in that very bosom he has wounded; he shall find the blood he shed an ample atonement for the sin of shedding it; and tell him from me, he will put me to more pain by refusing this offer of my blood than when first he drew it forth.'

O blessed Jesus, is this thy heart of love? Lift up thy prayer anew over the writer and the readers of these pages, 'Father, forgive them.'

Oh, my fellow-sinners, lift up a prayer for yourselves, for, as Augustine has it, 'Mercy prayed that misery might pray; the physician prayed that the sick might pray; the judge, willing to be merciful, prayed that the guilty might plead to be spared.'

'Our Father, which art in heaven, … forgive us our trespasses.'

II

Lord, remember me when thou comest into thy kingdom. Verily, I say unto thee, Today shalt thou be with me in Paradise.

When to the cross I turn mine eyes
  And rest on Calvary,
O Lamb of God, my sacrifice,
  I must remember Thee.
And when these failing lips grow dumb,
  And mind and memory flee;
When Thou shalt in Thy kingdom come,
  Jesus, remember me.

II

Lord, remember me when thou comest into thy kingdom.
Verily, I say unto thee, Today shalt thou be with me in Paradise.—LUKE 23: 42, 43

THE Saviour hangs in silence on the tree. A voice of mockery
is heard from one of the crosses at his side; but from the
other the voice of prayer, a voice sweeter in the sufferer's ear
than if a ministering angel had whispered peace, the voice of
one saved by his blood at his very side, the firstfruits of his
great redemption, as bright a jewel in his crown as any saved
before or since.

I. I note the word of the dying thief.

I know not what special influences wrought on this man
to change such a sinner into such a saint. As he walked to
Calvary with Jesus, he would hear these words to the daugh-
ters of Jerusalem, the last preaching of repentance by the
prophet of Israel: 'Weep not for me, but weep for yourselves
and for your children; for if they do these things in a green
tree, what shall be done in the dry?' As he was nailed to
the tree by the Saviour's side, he would hear the prayer of
intercession from the great high priest, 'Father, forgive
them.' And in the whole bearing of that meek and lowly

one, there was a kingly glory which told a strange tale to any heart which heaven softened by its grace. The grand secret of the wondrous change on that sinner *on* the cross, as on any sinner *at* the cross, is the application by the Spirit to the mind and heart and conscience of the Redeemer's atoning blood. The mysterious change is there, on that cross on the right, in that poor sinner's heart, a change which God alone hath wrought, a change from darkness to light, from death to life, from the power of Satan to the love of God, a change which has in it the developing germs of a new life, a life to God which shall be eternal in the heavens. The change is there—penitence for sin is there—a broken heart is there—faith in the crucified as his Lord and King is there—*there*, ere a word is spoken, doubtless his heart is praying, and his soul is being prepared to meet his God!

The silence of the penitent is broken by the 'us' of his companion compromising him in the scoff, 'If thou be Christ, save thyself and *us*.' 'Us!' oh no! He must rebuke a scoffing prayer of impenitence and unbelief, and that mockery, a word which puts the Holy One between them on a level with evil-doers like themselves; he wonders that his old companion has now no fear of God and judgment, and no sympathy, to say the least, with a sufferer at his side, as if the mockeries around the cross were not enough. 'Dost not thou fear God (or dost not even thou fear God), seeing thou art in the same condemnation?' He frankly owns his sin as he calls his brother to repentance with him, and in that confession puts in a word to testify to the innocence and holiness of him in whom he now believes as a suffering *Saviour*, and not like them, a suffering *sinner*: 'We indeed justly, for we receive the due reward of our deeds, but this man hath done nothing amiss.'

Now the dying penitent turns to Jesus, for his hopes are centred all on him; his faith is growing fast, he is clinging to the Rock of Ages, and, committing his soul for eternity to the man in the crown of thorns at his side, he calls him 'Lord,' and asks to be remembered at his coming in his kingdom—'Lord, remember me when thou comest into thy kingdom,' or rather *in* thy kingdom, in thy glory, at thy coming in the glory of thy kingdom.

What a prayer! What faith! in such circumstances! from such a man! Does he see in that lowly head beneath the crown of thorns a head which shall wear one day a crown of glory? Does he see in the man whom the world has placed between two malefactors, the Lord and King of heaven? Does he believe that this dying one shall live again and come in glory to reign, and that his cross is the pathway to the crown? Does he, a rebel once against high heaven, own himself a subject now of Jesus the mediator King? All this he does! Oh! what heaven-imparted faith! what illumination from above amid the darkness of the scene of Calvary, and the darkness of a sinner's heart like his!

What distinguishing sovereign grace, when round the cross thousands of hearts are as dark as night, and on the left side another heart black as hell!—'Lord, remember me at thy coming in thy kingdom.'

And what touching humility mingles with the faith, 'Remember me.' He asks no special place. 'Not worthy to be called a son' may be even now the thought in his heart; and in the humility, what faith! To remember me will be enough. Lord, wilt thou just grant me this, that when thou comest forth as the glorious King, and thy sceptre rules, and earth is made thy dominion from sea to sea, and hearts and souls are thine, and thy glory is revealed in sight of heaven and earth, wilt thou just grant me this—that thou wilt not forget, but think upon the thief who once hung by thy side on Calvary—'Lord, remember me when thou comest in thy kingdom.'

II. I note the word of the dying Lord.

What first appears is the calm composure and holy confidence of the suffering King, dying with a crown of thorns on his brow, though he be Lord of all.

To the scoffing taunt of the malefactor on his left, he makes no reply. To the prayer which owns him as the Lord of a kingdom, he responds with authority in the full consciousness of his mediatorial lordship, 'Verily, I say unto thee.'

And how glorious is the grace in such a word as this, at such an hour, to such a man! It far exceeds the thought of the dying thief; *he* speaks of some uncertain 'when,'—of the period, perhaps far distant in the future, when that kingdom in which he now believes shall be revealed by him whose glory is now concealed beneath the thorny crown. The Lord replies—'*Today*,' this very day, ere the close of this natural day. 'Remember me,' prays the humble penitent. 'Thou shalt *be with me*,' replies the gracious King. 'Remember me *when* thou comest in thy kingdom.' '*Today* shalt thou be with me in paradise.'

Can we conceive the peace and joy in the soul of that saved one amid the agonies of a cross! Led as a malefactor to the tree, and dying there as a sinner, with dark thoughts perhaps of eternity, and without a hope; and heaven's light beginning to stream in upon his soul, discovering to him the Christ of God at his side, and in the mirror of a dying Saviour's love, his own heart of sin, till he feels the heart drawn out as by cords of love he never knew before, to the God at whose judgment bar he is so soon to stand!

Can we conceive the overpowering surprise to a newly-enlightened soul, by a sure word of promise of the opening of paradise for him that day, and the presence of the eternal King to be known that day, as the beginning of everlasting bliss! What a transition from a malefactor's cross, and the devil's service, to the presence and fellowship of Jesus in the paradise of God!—It is a comfortless doctrine, while unscriptural, that there is some intermediate state, a state of very partial bliss, of a kind of inactivity or sleep, waiting the glory at the final resurrection of the just. *Today* shalt thou be with me in paradise. Surely this is glory for the saved soul. Surely this is heaven! The only difference which Scripture sanctions between the immediate glory of departed saints and the glory of a more distant age, is, that the one is the glory of a soul in separation from the body which meanwhile sleeps in the dust of earth, and the other the glory of soul and body united; the one is the individual glory of the departed with Jesus, the other is the full glory of the kingdom when Christ shall be revealed and all his saints with him, and redemption work shall be finally accomplished, and the kingdom delivered up by the Son, to the glory of God the Father.

'Thou shalt be with me,' *that* makes heaven; the unveiled, unmarred, uninterrupted presence of Jesus, *that* is heaven. It is Paul's definition of heaven, as the heaven he looked for, 'To depart and be with Christ.' It is the heaven, the immediate heaven, promised to the dying thief, 'Thou shalt be *with me.*'

The word *paradise* was used generally to express future bliss. Thus the Jews used it, and with reference to the bliss of Eden, where there was no sorrow and no sin. It is not the full glory of the coming kingdom, when the believer dies, but still it is paradise. Paradise! to the redeemed soul, like that garden of bliss to unfallen man, where no thorns or thistles grow, where the soul is never sad, and the Father of love never absent, where no tears are shed, and no sighs are known, and no sorrow ever comes! Paradise! with the tree of life, and access to it free. Paradise, regained, regained as a home for the weary, and a refuge for the troubled, where the storms of life shall never rise, and the sins and sorrows of our pilgrimage cease for ever! It is the word of the Saviour to a saved sinner; the word of the dying Saviour to a dying sinner, 'Thou shalt be with me in paradise.' Oh! precious word for our dying day; a word which has made many a pillow soft, and many a sufferer calm, and many a chamber of death the gate of heaven! May it be ours to hear it when the summons comes to us to take in our sails for an entrance into an eternal haven! May it be ours to hear it when death draws near, and voices whisper in our ear some comfortable words for the dying! May it be ours to hear Jesus say, 'Today thou shalt be with me in paradise.'

Three crosses on Calvary, and 'Jesus in the midst.'

1. It is the place which *the world* gives to Jesus. What a world is this! What an unholy, ungrateful, unfeeling being is man; what an evidence is given in the world's treatment of Jesus, of its hatred of all that is pure and holy and Godlike! How he lived for men, and opened wide his heart and hand to bless them, and yet they hated him. See these two malefactors on the cross! the place which the world gives to Jesus is 'in the midst.'

And is the world changed? Would men nowadays not do an act like this? I ask, has the world received Jesus? Have you? for if not, this is crucifying him afresh, and giving him a deceiver's place, a malefactor's place, aye, making his God and Father a liar; 'because you believe not the record that God gave of his Son' (1 John 5:10).

2. It is the place which *God* gives to Jesus, 'Jesus in the midst.' Strange mystery this, and yet the mystery of redemption. It is the atonement for the sin of man by the Son of God. The eternal becomes incarnate to take imputed guilt, and taking it, he stands towards the law as a sinner—the law with its curse follows him, and follows him on to the accursed

tree between two thieves. What a sight is here!—Of man's sin! for the place which Jesus occupies is the sinner's place, under wrath's darkest frown and the law's heaviest curse.—Of God's justice! for his own Son, if he takes imputed guilt, must have the sinner's place—he spared him not.—Of God's love! Will he for the sinner's sake put his own Son in the sinner's place? Yes, his own Son between two thieves! 'God so loved the world, that he gave his only begotten Son' (John 3:16).

3. 'Jesus in the midst,' and of the two beside him one lost and the other saved. It is a picture of the world still, and of the bearing of the atonement on the world. The cross is in the midst. It has been raised on a sin-cursed earth, and in the gospel Jesus is still lifted up, crying as if with outstretched arms, as on his cross, to all around to look and live, to believe and be saved. But the world is divided. Some reject the atonement, others receive it. Some are lost, others are saved—Jesus is in the midst.

Would you be saved like the dying thief? There is blood to save. There is grace to save. The time is *now*!

Do any despair of mercy because their sins are so great, and their repentance so late? At the deathbed of any poor sinner, who seems as if in one brief hour he might dash on the rocks of an eternal shore and make shipwreck forever, tell the story of the dying thief.

Do any put off the salvation of their souls, and fancy that a little contrition and a deathbed prayer will make all right at last? Forget not that there is far more here in this dying thief than a mere sigh for mercy! There is here what no man can count upon, what no man can make for himself, a broken spirit, a contrite heart, an enlightened mind, a monument of Heaven's sovereign grace! And the men who never will become such, are in all likelihood the men who vainly, rashly count upon it as a thing only worth having when the world's work is done, and life's sinful pleasures have slipped all away. *Today, today* is the time. *Now, now*, is the hour. 'Behold now is the accepted time; behold now is the day of salvation' (2 Cor. 6:2).

> A Cross—and one who hangs thereon, in sight
> Of heaven and earth. …
> > But still again,
> And yet again, the weary eyes are raised
> To seek the face of ONE who hangeth pale
> > Upon another cross. …
> > He sees alone
> That Face upon the cross. Oh, long, long look,
> That searcheth there the deep and awful things
> Which are of God. …
> > At length
> The pale, glad lips have breathed the trembling
> > prayer,
> 'O Lord, remember me!'
> > Oh, strange and solemn joy,
> Which broke upon the fading face of him
> Who there received the promise: 'Thou shalt be
> In paradise this night, this night, with ME.'

'I look this day
On Him whom I have pierced, and mourn for Him
With bitter mourning. My countless sins
Are heavy on His head: I mourn for Him
Whom I have pierced. Behold, He loved me,
And gives Himself for me!'
Thus it was
That day on Calvary.
O Christ the King: we will not come to Thee
Till Thou hast nailed us to some bitter cross,
And *made* us look on Thine; and driven at last
To call on Thee with trembling and with tears,
Thou lookest down in love, upbraiding not,
And promising the kingdom!

III

When Jesus therefore saw his mother, and the disciple standing by whom he loved, he saith unto his mother, Woman, behold thy son! Then saith he to the disciple, Behold thy mother! And from that hour that disciple took her unto his own home.

Our hearts are faint with sorrow,
    Heavy and hard to bear,
For we dread the bitter morrow,
    But we will not despair;
Thou knowest all our anguish,
    And Thou wilt bid it cease.
O Lamb of God, who takest
The sin of the world away,
    Give us Thy Peace!

III

When Jesus therefore saw his mother, and the disciple standing by whom he loved, he saith unto his mother, Woman, behold thy son! Then saith he to the disciple, Behold thy mother! And from that hour that disciple took her unto his own home.—JOHN 19:26, 27

SILENT love stands near the dying one in his last hours of suffering. From the cross he sees the little group, and fastening eye and word specially on two of them, the beloved disciple, and his mother whose soul the predicted sword is piercing, he says, 'Woman, behold thy son!' and to the disciple, 'Behold thy mother!'

Both words bear on Mary his mother; the one for the comfort of her heart, and the other for the guidance of the beloved disciple in the delegated duties of love.

I. The word to his mother, 'Woman, behold thy son.'

Here is a picture, a most lovely one, of the *human love* of Jesus. It is 'a word of love spoken as a human son to a human mother.' He is dying as *the Saviour*, and as the Saviour he has spoken already from that cross a prayer for his murderers, in a word of saving blessing to the thief at his side, but now he speaks as a *Son*.

Ah! verily! that heart of his beats towards his mother as the heart of other sons, only the quicker, because, never was a heart so tender, never love so pure! and he knows how *her* heart beats towards *him*. And so on his cross, in his last hours, as the sword is piercing her poor soul, he will not, cannot forget her.

And what can he do? He has no legacy to leave, for, 'for our sakes he became poor,' and though he had, that would be a poor substitute for love! His very garments have been parted, the last vestige of what the Lord of all owned as the poor Nazarene! He cannot deal with his widowed mother as with the widow of Nain, whose son, borne to his grave, he gave back again to a weeping mother. If he is to save us and Mary too forever, he cannot give back himself, but instead he gives another son. Human love is interwoven in this whole dying transaction: 'When Jesus saw his mother, and the disciple standing by whom he loved, he saith unto his mother, Woman, behold thy son! and to the disciple, Behold thy mother! and from that hour that disciple took her unto his own home.'

It is a delicate but precious theme, the *human love* of Jesus. It is this, I think, we see in the case of the young man who came to him about eternal life, 'Jesus, beholding him, loved him' (Mark 10:21). It is this we see brought out in no more touching way than in the name which John gives himself, 'that disciple whom Jesus loved.' It is this which the family of Bethany so largely shared, of whom the story tells, 'Now Jesus loved Martha, and her sister, and Lazarus' (John 11:5).

It is this love which lives in death, as on his cross, amid the agonies of the tree, and the great work of redemption, he forgets not *his mother*!

Thank God that we are permitted to love!—that strong affections are not sinful!—that earthly ties are Christlike!—that human love need never die if it be in the Lord!—that even from our deathbeds as from his cross, and at deathbeds as at his cross, we all may do what Jesus and John and Mary did,—love on in death, love on though parting, love the absent, love as those who shall meet again where hearts are never broken and love is never wounded and tears are never shed!

The human heart feels this to be true comfort. And *in Jesus* it is so human-like, that it, as well as love divine, attracts me to him!

Human love! Oh! melancholy thing to have it in my heart, if it be wrong to cherish it!

Moderate that love! say some. But must an affection so tender, so Christlike, be ever kept in check, lest I too dearly love friends and kindred? It will make it easier to part! say others. Nay; for if the heart ceases to love, it dies! My only comfort lies in this, Love on! love ever!—love the absent!—love in death!—love those in heaven as but a little sooner home!—love with all thy might, only love God first and best, and you love like Jesus!

We know how in him natural relationship held a subordinate place to that which was spiritual, how in his case nothing of earth was allowed to interfere with the claims of heaven, nothing of nature permitted to retard the work of grace. From him we learn that earthly relationships, however dear, must never raise their claims above the work which the Lord has given us to do, must never come into competition with the service of God! When some came to him in the midst of his great spiritual work, and told him that his mother and brethren 'stood without, desiring to speak with him,' Jesus answered, 'Who is my mother? and who are my brethren?' and stretching forth his hand towards his disciples, said, 'Behold my mother and my brethren. For whosoever shall do the will of my Father which is in heaven, the same is my brother, and sister, and mother' (Matt. 12:46-50).

On the one side, it is true that God and heaven, and the soul, and spiritual and eternal interests, must hold the highest place, and have the first great claim on heart and life alike!

But on the other side, it is a great, a comforting truth, that no feelings of human affection are destroyed or weakened by religion, but rather deepened, intensified, only regulated and sanctified! The heart loves still as ever, and it is its life to love, but with a purer, holier, more tender love. Just as on the one side you must not allow the dearest relationships of life, the fondest human affection, to interfere with your work for God, so on the other your work for God will never lead you to neglect the sacred duties of common life, of earthly love!

Think not that God requires at your hand active service for him away from your home, if in your home the duties of earthly love are to remain undone. Some have thus neglected home work, and brought a scandal on religion. Some have so busied themselves with outside work, as to forget that they have homes to care for, and a most precious field, though limited, at their own fireside. I own that such cases are exceptional, that far more common is the class who do little work in the world for God, who forget that at their doors are perishing souls, and all around in God's world are the lost and the dying,—men, women, and children needing a helping hand to lead them to Jesus!

Still, let all kinds of work, and all duties, and all relationships have their right place. This is God's way and will for us. And thus, while I find that my Saviour allowed no earthly ties to interfere with his grand spiritual work, I also find that on his very cross, in the midst of his great, redeeming, atoning work and offering of himself to God, he paused a moment to comfort his mother's heart, and commit her in his dying hour to another son! 'Woman, behold thy son!'

II. The word to John. 'Behold thy mother.'

I have said that both the words in this third saying of Jesus on the cross, bear on the case of his mother. 'Woman, behold thy son,' is the word for the comfort of her heart, that she may feel she is not left alone, but committed to a heart of love, to the bosom of him who himself lay in the bosom of Jesus! 'Behold thy mother,' is the word for the guidance of John, in discharge of the delegated duties of love. It is not that he is to think of Mary as a mother to him, but of himself as called to be a son to her. 'Behold thy mother!' As if to say, and the look and simple word together tell it, Take care of her, for my sake do it, in my place do it.

And what is here brought to view but the precious thought that the Saviour, whose care was for soul and body, for all the interests of humanity, and especially the most desolate and needy, appoints in his absence deputies on earth to represent and discharge his loving care alike for the souls and bodies of men!

I view Mary first, in a spiritual aspect, as a believer in Jesus.

Though the Lord's mother as to his human nature, she needed for herself the same faith in him as a divine Saviour as other sinners, and she got it; *when* actually we know not; but during her strange earthly life and his, she laid up in her heart the wonderful words which came from his lips, and we doubt not the Spirit taught her to know him, and believe in him, as her own Saviour, even before she stood by his cross. At all events, we find her specially named among the disciples in the 'upper room' on the Day of Pentecost, assembled to pray for the Spirit from the risen Christ.

I view Mary besides as a type of the most helpless ones in the world, such as the widow, the orphan, the desolate, and all weary, heavy-laden ones, specially the Lord's own poor burdened ones. Ah, if any sorrow be pressing on thy poor soul, if any pang now rends thy heart, he has a very loving care for thee.

But the lesson here is for those, like John, to whom the desolate are committed. In John you have a type of the disciples of love; in John's mission, a picture of your mission, believer, of your work on earth. It is to take the place of Jesus, as far as you possibly may, to be his deputy, his substitute, his steward here.

Think what a life was his! a life of constant well-doing, a life of care for the sorrowful and concern for the desolate and helpless! A life of active beneficence, in which he made the widow's heart to be glad, and the mourner to be comforted, and the poor to be relieved, and the perishing to be sought out and saved!

It is a grand idea, which you may not forget but seek to realise the more, that if you are a Christian, you are, in one great sense, in Christ's place here—left in that place by him— entrusted by him with the very work he did when himself was here! How little do many Christians think of this! How far short their conduct comes of that of the beloved disciple of whom it is recorded, 'From that hour that disciple took her to his own home.'

With many who profess the name of Christ, it is at best a passing good wish for the poor and the perishing, a cold distant sympathy, a coin tossed into another's hand from the lap of ease and comfort, to be given to the destitute, accompanied perhaps by complaints of the many calls and the large sacrifices they have made and the improvidence of the poor, and the worthlessness of the perishing!

Oh! if the kingdom of Jesus is soon to come, and the spirit of Jesus, and of John, who caught it direct from that altar of God, is to be seen on this earth of ours, we need far more tender love, and far more patient endurance, and far more self-denying effort. It is needed that, like John, Christians take the place of Jesus, and mingle with a sinful, suffering world, and take on themselves a part of the woes of the sorrowful, and enter by sympathising effort into the miseries of a sin-oppressed race of sufferers. Nothing so saddens one's heart, as to see how Christians sometimes stand aloof from the homes and haunts which Jesus would have visited, and the perishing ones *he* would have sought out to save.

And not a more refreshing sight can be seen than that of Christian men and women dealing their bread to the hungry, bringing the poor to their house, going down in sympathy to the most needy and desolate, bearing in their hands and on their lips the gospel of Jesus, and trying in their own humble way to act the Saviour's part. 'Pure religion, and undefiled, before God and the Father, is this, To visit the fatherless and widows in their affliction, and to keep himself unspotted from the world' (James 1:27).

While this is a lovely sight because it is Christlike, nothing so wins and gains a heart; sympathising love will do it, and will break down barriers, which all the cold and calculating schemes of mere professors, who would not touch the work with one of their little fingers, will fail to reach! You may well talk of '*cold charity*,' if in your comfortable position in which God hath placed you, you forget that it is he who hath done it, and with a patronising air cast a little help, not unmingled with reproach, to be picked up by the unfortunate, the desolate, the poor, the outcast.

Personal, self-denying, self-sacrificing, sympathising love and effort, this God asks of thee, if thou art a Christian; this Jesus asks thee to do *for him*, and *as like him as you can do it*, and this he will reckon *as done to him*! 'Freely ye have received, freely give!' (Matt. 10:8). Happy the man or the woman who can humbly say, 'When the ear heard me, then it blessed me; and when the eye saw me, it give witness to me; because I delivered the poor that cried, and the fatherless, and him that had none to help him. The blessing of him that was ready to perish came upon me: and I caused the widow's heart to sing for joy. I was eyes to the blind, and feet was I to the lame. I was a father to the poor; and the cause which I knew not I searched out' (Job 29:11-16). Happy they who shall at last hear the voice of Jesus saying, 'Come, ye blessed of my Father, inherit the kingdom: for I was an hungered, and ye gave me meat: I was thirsty, and ye gave me drink: I was a stranger, and ye took me in: naked, and ye clothed me: I was sick, and ye visited me: I was in prison, and ye came unto me. … Inasmuch as ye have done it unto one of the least of these my brethren, ye have done it unto me' (Matt. 25:34-40).

> The strongest light casts deepest shade,
>   The dearest love makes dreariest loss;
> And she His birth so blessed had made,
>   Stood by Him dying on the cross.
>
> Yet since not grief but joy shall last,
>   The day and not the night abide,

And all time's shadows, earthward cast,
  Are lights upon the other aide;

Through what long bliss that shall not fail,
  That darkest hour shall brighten on!
Better than any angel's 'Hail'!
  The memory of 'Behold thy son.'

IV

And at the ninth hour Jesus cried with a loud voice, saying, Eloi, Eloi, lama sabachthani? which is, being interpreted, My God, my God, why hast thou forsaken me?

Yea once Immanuel's orphan cry
    His universe hath shaken,
It went up single, echoless,
    'My God, I am forsaken,'
It went up from the Holy's lips
    Amid His lost creation
That of the lost no son should use
    Those words of desolation.

IV

And at the ninth hour Jesus cried with a loud voice, saying, Eloi, Eloi, lama sabachthani? which is, being interpreted, My God, My God, why hast thou forsaken me?—MARK 15:34.

IT was the darkest, yet the brightest, day the world ever saw!

Never was such a deed of darkness as the crucifixion of the Lord of glory—never was such a sufferer as the Son of God when he hung upon the accursed tree. Never such dismal hours as when there was darkness, not only over all the land, but darkness in the soul of the Father's well-beloved, when a veil was drawn between, and the light of Heaven's love was all eclipsed. Who can realise the depth of suffering, and the agony of desertion, that drew forth the cry, 'My God, my God, why hast thou forsaken me?' It was the darkest day the world ever saw!

But how the brightest?

Ah, the brightest! because there shone forth, in fullest manifestation, the love of God to a lost and ruined world.

It was *dark to Jesus* that it might be *bright to us*. The Father forsook him that we might not be forsaken to all eternity.

From the shame of Jesus we get our glory; from his sufferings we get salvation; from his wounds we get our healing; from the wrath on him we get our peace; by his death we live!

If in the scene of the crucifixion this be the darkest part in the dark picture, then from it there may shine to us the brightest light. In that Father's frown we may see a smile, in the forsaken one believers may see themselves brought nigh; and as they hear from their Saviour's lips the awful words, 'My God, my God, why hast thou forsaken me?' they may also hear a God of love declaring to every ransomed one, to every soul that believes in Jesus, 'I will never leave thee, nor *forsake thee*, to all eternity' (Heb. 13:5).

In viewing this strange and solemn scene, the abandonment or desertion of Jesus, I note—

I. The nature of it.

And here we require to bear in mind the mystery of the person of the sufferer.

He who hangs on the cross, and exclaims, 'My God, my God, why hast thou forsaken me?' is the Son of God and the Son of man! Mysterious union this of natures, the divine and human in one person; 'Great is the mystery of godliness, God manifest in the flesh' (1 Tim. 3:16), the Son of God assuming human nature, and in that nature obeying, suffering, and dying on the cross. The world sees in him, and his murderers see in him, only a despised Nazarene. But, ah! within that man there is a holy human soul, and beneath the garb of humanity is the Son of God—'We beheld his glory, the glory as of the only begotten of the Father, full of grace and truth' (John 1:14).

And although it was only in his humanity that he could suffer, for the divinity cannot suffer—he only that hath immortality cannot die—yet between these two natures there is a marvellous and indescribable union, so that when it is asked, Who is this on Calvary? the answer is, It is the Son of God, it is the Son of man, it is our divine Redeemer, who yet, as you see, is bone of our bone and flesh of our flesh!

Now when Jesus cried upon the cross, 'My God, my God, why hast thou forsaken me?' he meant not that anything was affecting the union between the divine and human natures. Such a union having been formed, the eternal Son having taken our nature into personal union with himself, nothing can dissolve, nothing can disturb, this union; and it was as the God-man Redeemer that he cried, 'My God, my God, why hast thou forsaken me?'

Neither are we to suppose that when Jesus uttered this mournful cry, the love of the Father towards him had ceased or abated in the slightest degree. The Father loves the Son, and he cannot cease to love him. His love is eternal as himself, unchangeable as his own divine nature; and had it been possible for the love of the Father to the Son to have increased, I believe it would have been when 'he took the form of a servant' (Phil. 2:7), when he stooped so low as to become a man, and 'became obedient unto death, even the death of the cross' (Phil. 2:8). Yea, Jesus himself tells us,

'Therefore doth my Father love me, because I lay down my life, that I might take it again' (John 10:17).

Neither are we to imagine that when this cry was uttered, 'My God, my God, why hast thou forsaken me?' there was a withdrawal of the support which the Divinity had ever given to the suffering Saviour. God had said, Go, my Son, and I will hold thy hand; and even when Jesus was forsaken on the cross, God could say, 'Behold my servant whom I uphold' (Isa. 42:1), with respect to the actual support which was given even then, and without which there never had been a suffering and victorious Saviour.

What, then, was this awful desertion?

There is in it a depth of gloom and horror which it is difficult, aye, impossible, for the human mind to fathom and fully comprehend. God withdraws from Jesus the light of his countenance, the comfortable sense of his love and his complacency in him. He makes him to feel the whole weight of wrath lying upon him as the sinner's substitute and surety; and whereas the weight of this wrath is only completely felt when God's absence is felt—when one is made to know the horror of being alone—in God's universe without God—when the light of heaven is altogether eclipsed, and when one stands as forgotten, cast off, forsaken, Jesus is made to feel it thus, and so to utter the doleful cry, 'My God, my God, why hast thou forsaken me!'

He was never left thus alone before. Forsaken by all others, we never saw him forsaken by his Father; but now he is emphatically the forsaken one, hanging between earth and heaven, as if owned by neither—'Cast out from earth as a curse, and not yet received to blessing in heaven.' Heaven and earth and hell all against him! Once we hear him crying, 'Now is my soul troubled, and what shall I say?' (John 12:27), but from heaven there comes a voice to comfort him; and though all around is dark, when he looks up, there is light in heaven and love in the Father's eye. We hear him in Gethsemane pouring forth strong cries and tears, and agonising as the bloody sweat falls on the ground, and the prayer ascends, 'Father, if it be possible, let this cup pass from me' (Matt. 26:39), but there is an open ear in heaven to hear that prayer, and a swift messenger wings his way to comfort and strengthen the suffering one. But at the dark hour when he hung on the cross there was no voice from heaven, no messenger—aye, no light, darkness over all the earth, and deeper darkness in the Messiah's soul.

Behold on the cross the forsaken one!

II. The *reason* of the abandonment or desertion of Jesus.

Why is it so? Why has the God of love forsaken his beloved Son? How many an adopted child of God has died in peace, enjoying on his deathbed the light and love of Heaven, and singing on earth the song of the New Jerusalem! How many a martyr has expired triumphantly amid the flames, and rejoiced in the presence and support of the God he loved! It was with them the season of sweetest, richest consolation. Underneath and around they felt the everlasting arms, and they saw with faith's clear eye the face of God, and had poured into their souls celestial light; and why—oh! why is the well-beloved, the only-begotten, the dearest Son expiring in the thickest darkness, feeling nought but the Father's frown?

In the explanation of the mystery we have the gospel of the grace of God. In the suffering Jesus we see the sinner's substitute and surety. Out of love to souls God delivered him up to the death of the cross, and he suffered our punishment while he 'bore our sins in his own body on the tree' (1 Pet. 2:24). We have forsaken God; we have left our Father's home, like the poor, wandering prodigal; and the fruit of the sinner's sin in forsaking God is that God forsakes him. Thus by sin we are cut off from God—from his favour, from his love, from his blessing, from all communion with him. And if you ask for the darkest picture of a forsaken sinner, of one reaping the bitter fruits of departure from his God, I point to the place of woe where there is 'wailing and gnashing of teeth' (Matt. 13:50). On the lost in hell lies the wrath of God, and who can tell the horror of falling thus into the hands of an angry God? But with this felt wrath and curse, there is the awful sense of God's eternal absence.

Ah! they are banished ones; they have heard the sentence, 'Depart from me, ye cursed!' (Matt. 25:41). Nevermore shall ye see my face, never feel my favour, never know my smile, but down, deep down in the dark prison-house shall be your eternal home! Thou hast forsaken me! is the eternal shriek of a lost soul. Thou hast forsaken me, I am left alone! I am undone, for ever undone; for thou art absent, save in thine awful presence as a God of wrath and a God of terror, looking on me with thine eternal frown!

Jesus is the banished one in your room and stead, O *believing sinner*! When he was forsaken on the cross, this was part of his suffering for you. He must taste the bitterest ingredient in the cup of wrath. He must drink of that cup to the very dregs; and as we deserved to be cast off, abandoned, forsaken to all eternity, see on the cross the banished one, the Son of God in darkness, gloom, and woe.

Behold on the cross the forsaken one!

III. The *suffering* in the abandonment or desertion of Jesus.

Intense must have been the agony of soul when Jesus uttered such a cry. Why is it so? was a question never asked before by him. 'He was led as a lamb to the slaughter; and as a sheep before his shearers is dumb, so he opened not his mouth' (Isa. 53:7). All the cruelties of his enemies, all the unkindness of his friends, drew forth no sorrow, no complaint at all equal in intensity to this. Here is the bitterest portion of the cup of wrath, here is the sharpest wound of the sword of justice. And he who opened not his mouth like a lamb, now roars like a lion, as that word means which we have in Psalm 22, 'My God, my God, why hast thou forsaken me? why art thou so far from helping me, and from the words of my roaring?'

To realise at all the intensity of the suffering of Jesus at this awful hour, you have to bear in mind that this is but the consummation of the sufferings of his life. He was 'a man of sorrows' (Isa. 53:3) all his days—'Foxes have holes, and the birds of the air have nests, but the Son of man hath not where to lay his head' (Luke 9:58). One disciple has denied him; another has betrayed him; and when he was led away to the high priest's house, they all forsook him and fled. His enemies have been treating him as the vilest malefactor; and amid shame and mocking and cruel violence, they have hurried him away to Golgotha. There is one shout which comes from a united rabble—'Away with him, away with him! crucify him, crucify him!' (Luke 23:18, 21). He is weary and worn with suffering. It has told on his very countenance, which is 'more marred than that of any man' (Isa. 52:14); and when little more than thirty, men take him for fifty; and at last, when stretched on the cross, and looking at his emaciated frame, he exclaims, 'I can tell' (I can count) 'all my bones!' (Psa. 22:17).

See him now on the cross. That cry, 'My God, my God, why hast thou forsaken me?' was uttered when he seemed given over to the malice of his cruel foes. For a time, the chains that bind and restrain the spirits of darkness are loosened, and they rage and riot around that cross. See their cruel and malicious enmity as cherished in the breasts and exhibited in the words and deeds of the savage murderers. No taunts are spared, no act of cruelty is wanting; it seems to be their aim to sport with the agonising Saviour. Do you not think you see them dividing his garments when they have nailed him to the cross, and sitting down to watch him there? But they cannot rest: it is too mild a death to allow him to expire without an addition of suffering inflicted by the hands that have nailed him to the tree. They pass and repass, and mock and revile and blaspheme, 'wagging their heads, and saying, If thou be the Son of God, come down from the cross: he saved others, himself he cannot save' (Matt. 27:35, 36, 39, 40, and Mark 15:29-32).

And then, who can tell how fierce that conflict was, unseen by man, with the powers of darkness! The prince of this world comes to meet the Prince of Peace; Golgotha is the battlefield, and on the cross is the end of the awful conflict. But who can tell how fierce it was, when with the powers of darkness it was the last struggle to defeat the purposes of God, and ruin the souls of men!

At this awful hour, when deserted by friends, and insulted and wounded by enemies, and wrestling with the prince of darkness for a world of sinners—at this awful hour the Father leaves him, hides the light of his countenance, and lets fall the full and to us inconceivable impression of the wrath due to the sinners for whom he dies. He makes our iniquities to meet on him, and forsakes him!

Can we at all comprehend the agony, the gloom, of these three awful hours? Wrapt in darkness deeper far than that which covered the earth (for that was but the symbol and the image of the internal darkening of the sufferer's soul), he agonises under the hiding of his Father's countenance; his holy soul is filled with woe; and under the pressure of the suffering, which our words fail to describe, and our minds scarce can comprehend, he cries, 'My God, my God, why hast thou forsaken me?'

Behold on the cross the forsaken one!

IV. The *fruit* of the abandonment or desertion of Jesus.

I have said that the crucifixion day was the darkest, yet the brightest, the world ever saw.

It is now, it will be to all eternity, the darkest day to some, the brightest day to others. To the lost in hell it stands out in awful horror as the darkest day in the world's history. To the saved in heaven it stands forth in lofty grandeur as the brightest day. The cross has a dark and a bright side. From it comes terror. From it comes consolation. By the same awful scenes it proclaims wrath and peace; and in them we read of damnation and salvation, of hell and heaven.

Look at the dark side first. In that forsaken one, in the abandonment of Jesus, you see a picture of hell. You see your merited curse. You see God's righteous wrath and holy indignation against sin. You see that the time is coming when all the impenitent and unbelieving shall be eternally cast away, forgotten, forsaken, lost. When you see in the cross of Christ and in the agonies of the forsaken Jesus a picture of sin's deserts, you learn that God is in earnest when he tells you what must be the bitter fruit and the eternal wages of sin. It is no mere threat. It is no empty declaration of vengeance that will never be realised. 'If they do these things in a green tree, what shall be done in the dry?' (Luke 23:31). In the abandonment of Jesus we hear the sentence ringing, 'Depart from me, ye cursed, into everlasting fire, prepared for the devil and his angels!' (Matt. 25:41). And if any of us are lost, verily the fruit of Christ's abandonment will be the aggravation of our misery, the increase of our doom; and the bitterest ingredient in the cup of wrath will be the never-ceasing thought that hell might have been escaped, that we had the offer made us of the merits of the sufferings of Jesus the forsaken one. 'How shall we escape, if we neglect so great salvation?' (Heb. 2:3).

Look now at the bright side of the cross.

What mercy and love and grace are to be seen in the face of Jesus Christ as he hangs on Calvary as the forsaken one! What hope for you, O anxious, trembling, yet believing souls! Jesus is forsaken that you may be received as returning prodigals to the Father's bosom and the Father's love, and never be forsaken to all eternity. Ye may come and lay your sins by faith on the head of the forsaken one. Ye may look on him as standing in your room and stead when the pains of hell gat hold upon him, and the Father's face was hid. What a mystery is here! What a dark, deep, gloomy gulf this seems—the desertion of Jesus on the cross—but come and bring all your sins and sorrows and fears and distresses, and bury them in this unfathomable gulf, and take peace and consolation in the thought that Jesus was the forsaken one for you, that the Father's answer to the Saviour's piercing cry, 'My God, my God, why hast thou forsaken me,' is his word of peace to the believing soul, 'I will never leave thee, nor forsake thee' (Heb. 13:5).

Is it not strange, the darkest hour
That ever dawned on sinful earth,
Should touch the heart with softer power
For comfort than an angel's mirth!

V

I thirst!

Thou wilt feel all, that Thou mayest pity all;
And rather wouldst thou wrestle with strong pain
    Than overcloud thy soul
    So clear in agony,
Or lose one glimpse of heaven before the time!
    O most entire and perfect Sacrifice,
    Renewed in every pulse
    That on the tedious cross
Told the long hours of death, as one by one
The life-strings of that tender heart gave way!

V

I thirst!—JOHN 19:28.

WONDROUS grace it is that the living waters for the weary sons of men flow from the cross of Calvary—that the invitation to us to drink abundantly has its secret and its power in the word which Jesus spake when the parching thirst of death was on him.

Oh, dig down, deep down into this word of Calvary, and you shall find there the well of water which shall quench your thirsty souls, if only you believe in the crucified one! And meanwhile, let me write over the word of Jesus, 'I thirst!' as the last word of Scripture to be accomplished in him ere he dies, the latest word of woe and weariness which fell from his blessed lips: let me write over it, and your hearts and mine utter it—'Herein is love' (1 John 4:10).

I. I take the word *literally*, as one which has often come from the lips of suffering and dying men.

What is in it in the case of Jesus?

1. I point to *the physical suffering*. No wonder that he was athirst! Was ever suffering like his?—mental, spiritual, added to the physical! To enter at all into it, you must

keep in mind that this is the Lord of glory—the Son of the Eternal incarnate—bearing the guilt of men and enduring the contradiction of sinners against himself, and the Father's face obscured because sin, in the form of imputed guilt, is on him!

Was ever suffering like his concentrated into four and twenty hours? Even on his way to his cross, how worn and weary was he, after not only the buffeting and mockery and haste of trial and condemnation, but the bloody sweat of Gethsemane, and the agony and the wrestling prayer! For hours he has hung on the cross, enduring not only the most exquisite bodily pain, but mockery from man, and temptation from devils, and the hiding of his Father's face, and through it all feeling the burden of the sin he bore, and caring with his tender heart for friends and foes, for the thief at his side, and his mother's pierced soul, and the salvation of all to the end of time, for whom he then was dying! His frame is fevered, his tongue cleaves to his jaws, and his burning lips would fain have a drop of water. 'I thirst!' 'My strength is dried up like a potsherd, and my tongue cleaveth to my jaws, and thou hast brought me into the dust of death' (Psa. 22:15).

And what an anguish is thirst! keener far than hunger; and we shudder at the stories travellers tell of their sufferings on the burning sands, when they would fain give all they own in the world for a few drops of water!

It is not without deep and emphatic meaning that in our Lord's parable of the sufferings of the lost he pictures the rich man praying that Lazarus might be allowed to 'dip the tip of his finger in water, and cool his tongue' (Luke 16:24). Jesus cried, 'I thirst!'

2. But besides the extremity of the physical suffering of Jesus, expressed in a word which tells the agony which dying mortals have in measure often felt, see here *the depth of humiliation and woe*; for who is this that cries on a cross, 'I thirst?'

It is the Lord of heaven; it is the Prince of life; it is he whose is the earth and the fulness thereof; it is he who made the ocean and opened the fountains of the deep, and guides in their course the rolling rivers, and showers the rain of heaven on the parched earth, and satisfies the desire of every living thing; it is *he* who cries, 'I thirst!'

Ah! there is far more here than what tells of his real humanity, as does his sleeping in a storm, and his weeping at a grave, and his resting as a weary man at Jacob's well, and asking there a drink of water. For in the cry—not uttered, mark ye, till he has suffered all, fulfilled all—in the cry, 'I thirst!' there is an indirect request to his very enemies round his cross, to his crucifiers. It is the Maker of the world crying to the world for one drop of water—'I thirst!'

3. Now, in the case of Jesus, *why* this depth of humiliation and woe? Why this extremity of suffering? Does it tell what sin is? Does it speak of sin's desert?

Does it picture *hell*? It does. The forsaken one between heaven and earth, a picture of the lost soul, forsaken for ever! 'I thirst!'—the eternal cry of the eternally parched, whose thirst is never quenched—of the eternally dying, who never die!

But ah! does it tell of *salvation*? Does the mystery of Jesus forsaken tell me I need never be? Does the sight of Jesus thirsting, and the cry for a drop of water from his lips, tell me that for me, a sinner at his cross, there is a fountain of living water? It does.

Oh, this is the divine mystery of Heaven's wisdom, of God's redeeming love, that light springs out of darkness, glory out of shame, life out of death, and the water of life from the parched lips of my dying Saviour!

Yes, it is that word, that last suffering word of my dying Lord, that last word of prophetic Scripture which remained for him to utter—it is that which gives the depth of meaning and the secret of power, and the efficacy to save to such a gospel word as his own in the days of his flesh—'If any man thirst, let him come unto me and drink' (John 7:37), to such a gospel word as the consummating invitation of the Bible from the lips of the glorified Jesus—'The Spirit and the bride say, Come; and let him that heareth say, Come; and let him that is athirst come: and whosoever will, let him take the water of life freely' (Rev. 22:17). Dig down, deep down into this word of Calvary, 'I thirst!' and you shall find there the well of water which shall quench the thirsty souls of all who but believe in the crucified one—'I will take the cup of salvation, and call on the name of the Lord' (Psa. 116:13). 'Therefore with joy shall ye draw water out of the wells of salvation' (Isa. 12:3). 'Drink, yea, drink abundantly' (Song of Sol. 5:1).

II. I take the word *spiritually*.

I do not venture to assert that in his own consciousness our Lord attached a spiritual meaning to the word. Enough, perhaps, that we have the deep spiritual truth already indicated rising out of and taught by the physical suffering which the word first denotes.

But then, what was it, I ask, that led the Redeemer down so low as this physical need? Was it not the thirst of his soul? Was it not the zeal for God and God's house which consumed him? Was it not intense longing for the Father's glory and the redemption of the lost which led him to this world, to that cross, which brought him down so low as to that awful physical thirst? It was.

And so in that bodily thirst I see, as it were, the outgoing of the thirst of his soul. Yes, as we penetrate to that which caused all his woe and all his manifestation of suffering love, we cannot fail to think of this deep spiritual thirst—thirst for God!—thirst for man!

Thirst for God! 'Lo, I come: I delight to do thy will, O my God' (Psa. 40:7, 8). 'My meat is to do the will of him that sent me, and to finish his work' (John 4:34). 'I have a baptism to be baptized with, and how am I straitened till it be accomplished!' (Luke 12:50). 'Father, the hour is come; glorify thy Son, that thy Son also may glorify thee' (John 17:1).

For the accomplishment of redemption work, for the Father's glory, he longs! Aye more, *the forsaken one* cries, 'I thirst!' For a sense of the Father's presence and the Father's love he longs! For the Father's home he longs! 'My God, my God, why hast thou forsaken me?' 'I thirst!' 'My soul thirsteth for thee, my flesh longeth for thee in a dry and parched land, where no water is' (Psa. 63:1). 'I stretch forth my hands unto thee: my soul thirsteth after thee, as a thirsty land' (Psa. 143:6).

Thirst for man! Thirst for souls. For this he lived; for this he dies. 'Come unto me, come unto me!' this was his life-cry. 'Ye will not come unto me that ye might have life' (John 5:40), this was his one complaint. 'Oh that thou hadst known, even thou, at least in this thy day, the things which belong unto thy peace! but now they are hid from thine eyes' (Luke 19:42), was his word as he wept over Jerusalem, and the depth of his thirst was for our salvation when he bled on Calvary!

Ah! if in one aspect of the cry 'I thirst!' there is an appeal to the world for help, an appeal from the world's Creator for a drop of water; in another aspect of it may there not be a last appeal to that poor world itself to listen to his longing love? Will any heart be moved ere he cries the great loud cry, 'It is finished!' will any one listen to his voice, 'I thirst?'

He is thirsting still, my fellow-sinners, for you—thirsting for your love—thirsting for your souls. For this—for this, my fellow-sinners, Jesus thirsts.

What a sight are these parched lips of the dying Jesus! What a volume of meaning in the brief word, more for meditation than exposition!

Omit not to note that his utterance of it was a fulfilment of prophetic Scripture, and the last that remained to be accomplished ere he died.

Omit not to note that Jesus the sufferer knew all—knew the unfolding of Scripture in his own case—knew it even as he hung on the tree—knew all and watched all, and suffered all and accomplished all, and caused his very crucifiers to fulfil their prophetic destiny in giving him vinegar to drink—'They gave me also gall for my meat, and in my thirst they gave me vinegar to drink' (Psa. 69:21). Well may we say—

> Oh for a pencil dipped in heavenly light,
> To paint the agonies which Jesus bore!

Shall this dying word of Jesus gain any heart?

1. Does it not let me know what is worth thirsting for? Not the pleasures of earth, not its wealth or honour; not the unsubstantial joys which can never fill a soul and never satisfy its craving;—not these, not these, but God's glory and salvation, our own and others.

2. Does Jesus thirst for me, for my soul, for my love—and shall I not thirst for him? Shall not the thought of his longing after me awaken in my cold heart a longing love for him? 'As the hart panteth after the water-brooks, so panteth my soul after thee, O God' (Psa. 42:1).

Finally, to sum all up again. There is living water for you, because Jesus thirsted. There is life for you, because Jesus died. Oh that the sight might be seen of Jesus beside you, meeting you, saving, satisfying your soul, as he met and satisfied and saved the woman of Sychar by Jacob's well!

Ah, my fellow-sinner! if thou knewest the gift of God—if thou wilt but know now, that Jesus, God's own Son, given for you, thirsted on Calvary's bitter tree, thirsted for thy sake, thirsted for thee, thou wilt 'ask of him, and he will give thee living water' (John 4:10).

Oh that the same voice might be heard by some hearts now which fell on the ears of a careless multitude on the last, the great day of the feast, when he who was so soon to thirst on Calvary, 'stood and cried, saying, If any man thirst, let him come unto me and drink' (John 7:37).

What should hinder? what should prevent the blessing, when Divine Love has given the Eternal Son, and Incarnate Love has wept and bled, and thirsted, and died, and from his throne in glory the same Jesus lifts his voice in words now written on the Bible's closing page—'I, Jesus, have sent mine angel to testify unto you these things in the churches. I am the root and the offspring of David, and the bright and morning star. And the Spirit and the bride say, Come. And let him that heareth say, Come. And let him that is athirst come; and whosoever will, let him take the water of life freely' (Rev. 22:16, 17).

VI

It is finished!

'Tis finished!—was His latest voice;
　These sacred accents o'er,
He bowed His head, gave up the ghost,
　And suffered pain no more.

'Tis finished!—the Messiah dies
　For sins, but not His own;
The great redemption is complete,
　And Satan's power o'erthrown.

'Tis finished!—all His groans are past,
　His blood, His pain, and toils,
Have fully vanquishèd our foes,
　And crowned Him with their spoils.

'Tis finished!—legal worship ends,
　And gospel ages run;
All old things now are past away,
　And a new world begun.

VI

It is finished!—John 19:30.

''Tis finished!—was His latest voice.' Not, after all, the latest, for there was one later still, in which, in his Father's arms, he breathed his soul away—'Father, into thy hands I commend my Spirit.'

But it is so near the Saviour's end—so very near, that if he is to *tell* that all is over, this is the latest moment for it.

Who can estimate the fulness and the bearing of the word? It is one word in the original, one word loudly spoken, as the shout of victory—victory when dying, victory through the death just coming.

Every time we read it, every time we take it up for solemn thought, we find in it new depths of meaning. Through eternity we shall be trying to fathom it, and find it infinite.

'It is finished!'—the finite mind cannot grasp the wide expanse over which a word like this extends—the human eye cannot take in the view. It is God's Son, the world's Redeemer, in fulfilment of eternal counsels of love divine, which overshadows a world of sinners, and reaches forward to the glory of eternity beyond—it is God's Son made a curse on an accursed tree, with outstretched arms, as if pointing to the eternal past and the eternal future, and open wide to embrace in his heart of love a world of sinners—it is God's Son, just ere he dies, crying with a loud voice, meant for all ages, and the very ends of the earth, and its echo for heaven and hell and eternity—this, and far more than I can possibly express, is in the word, 'It is finished!'

I. Manifestly the first bearing of the word is on *Scripture accomplished*.

I take this loud cry from the lips of the dying one as the proclamation of the fact that all the intimations of Scripture, whether in promise, or type, or prophecy, regarding the Messiah, have *in him* been accomplished—fulfilled.

It is written, 'Jesus, knowing that all things were now accomplished, that the Scripture might be fulfilled (or accomplished), saith, I thirst!' and then when he had received the vinegar, he cried, 'It is finished!' The meaning evidently is, that Jesus knew at that time that only one prediction in Scripture remained to be fulfilled in him before his death, namely, that one which told of his thirst, and of vinegar being given him to drink—'In my thirst they gave me vinegar to drink'; and so, having cried, in the extremity of wearied nature, 'I thirst!' and having received the vinegar, as nothing more remained to be fulfilled—as all that was written in Moses and in the Prophets and in the Psalms concerning him was accomplished, down to the last drops of vinegar to his lips, in the parched thirst of death, he cried, 'It is finished!'

What a strange but minute delineation do the Old Testament Scriptures give of the suffering Messiah! Surely it is a portrait which must infallibly make him known when he appears!

It is far on in the world's history ere God sends his Son. He might have sent him early, to die at once, and might have raised his cross near the very gates of Eden, and made the atonement an accomplished fact for the earliest age of the world and the church. But God had grand designs of his own in delaying the mission of his Son. To let the world feel itself alone, and the world's wisdom fail to find out God, and empty hearts learn that no device of man could fill the void.

But more than this, to give on the pages of revelation indications by prophecy and promise, and recorded types and ceremonies, such as would establish to ingenuous hearts the mission of Christ when he should appear; while, at the same time, was given by anticipation for the faith of the early believers a Christ and an atonement on which to rest—'The Lamb slain from the foundation of the world' (Rev. 13:8). Faint promises at first, becoming brighter and clearer as years roll on—old ceremonies designed to pass away—types whose significancy comes fully to view when they cease in the 'Lamb of God, which taketh away the sin of the world'! What a mark—what an unfailing mark of the Messiah, that all circumstances foretold must be fulfilled in him; circumstances, too, so numerous and so minute, and so mysteriously strange as the marks of heaven are, that it is beyond all possibility that they could meet in anyone but the real person! In Jesus of Nazareth they meet, and when this last prediction to be fulfilled ere he dies is accomplished, namely, the thirst and the vinegar, he cries, 'It is finished!' Glance for a moment at the minute fulfilment. I speak not of the types and ceremonies which on the pages of Scripture are recorded, and year by year in the past ages were witnessed in Israel's land. Take rather now these words from the Scriptures of both Testaments side by side:—

'They weighed for my price thirty pieces of silver' (Zech. 11:2).
'They covenanted with him for thirty pieces of silver' (Matt. 26:15).

'He was wounded' (Isa. 53:5).
'There they crucified him' (Luke 23:33).

'They shall look upon me whom they have pierced' (Zech. 12:10).
'One of the soldiers with a spear pierced his side' (John 19:34).

'They pierced my hands and my feet' (Psa. 22:16).
'Reach hither thy finger, and behold my hands: and reach hither thy hand, and thrust it into my side' (John 20:27).

'They part my garments among them, and cast lots upon my vesture' (Psa. 22:18).

'The soldiers took his garments, and made four parts, to every soldier a part; and also his coat: now the coat was without seam, woven from the top throughout. They said therefore among themselves, Let us not rend it, but cast lots for it, whose it shall be' (John 19:23).

'He was numbered with the transgressors' (Isa. 53:12). 'With him they crucify two thieves' (Mark 15:27).

'My God, my God, why hast thou forsaken me?' (Psa. 22:1).
'My God, my God, why hast thou forsaken me?' (Matt. 27:46).

'All they that see me laugh me to scorn: they shoot out the lip, they shake the head, saying, He trusted on the Lord that he would deliver him: let him deliver him, seeing he delighted in him' (Psa. 22:7, 8).
'They that passed by reviled him, wagging their heads, and saying, He trusted in God; let him deliver him now, if he will have him' (Matt. 27:39).

'In my thirst they gave me vinegar to drink' (Psa. 69:21).
'Jesus said, I thirst: and they filled a sponge with vinegar, and put it upon hyssop, and put it to his mouth' (John 19:28).

And when all was thus accomplished, when all the Scriptures concerning him were thus fulfilled, Jesus cried, 'It is finished!'

There are two important thoughts suggested here.

1. Jesus had an eye to the foundation of a sinner's faith, to the confirmation of the faith of disciples in all ages. This very evidence of the Messiahship he dwelt on afterwards in conversation with the two disciples on the way to Emmaus. 'Ought not Christ to have suffered these things, and to enter into his glory? And beginning at Moses and all the prophets, he expounded unto them in all the Scriptures the things concerning himself' (Luke 24:27).

2. The other thought is this—

All Scripture is one grand marvellous whole. Without the New Testament the Old is 'a riddle without its key, a beginning without an end.' The New is but an unveiling of the Old.

In Jesus they meet; in him they are united in spirit and truth and life more closely than the two Testaments within the boards of the Bible. The Christ who is the sum and substance of the gospel history, whose life and work and death are the burden of the story of the Evangelists, and the letters of the apostles; this Jesus Christ has his eye from his cross on the Old Scriptures, and says, 'It is finished! it is finished! In me they centre. In me they are all accomplished and fulfilled, down to this my dying hour.' And so, ere he breathes his soul away into his Father's hands, with loud voice he cries, 'It is finished!'

II. The second bearing of this word is on *the suffering work of his life as over.*

'It is finished!' I speak not of it now as a word which tells that the agonies of the greatest sufferer that ever lived are closing fast, that he has but to breathe out his soul, and the weary one is at rest. This, too, is in the word; and to him who was real man, and had a nature keenly sensitive, it must have been a joyous word in that dark hour, 'It is over now!' And in it, too, there must have been something of the joy of going home, out from a world like this, like that other word to his Father, 'And now I am no more in the world, I come to thee' (John 17:11).

But I take it now as telling of the work which the Father gave him to do for our salvation, of that work accomplished through suffering, immediately to be closed by the last act of dying, 'It is finished!'

One short Scripture word tells out that work, 'Obedient unto death' (Phil. 2:8). This is the mystery of the life and death of Jesus, the holy Son of God, in the room and place of guilty sinners, that Holy One working out for them a righteousness for their acceptance with their God!

Under the law, this is our place as *men*. Under the broken law, and therefore under its curse, this is our place as *sinners*. Let the incarnate Son of God take our place. *His* must be, *as man*, a holy, spotless, obedient life. *His* must be, as the *imputed Sin-bearer*, a suffering, accursed death!

The purity of that holy life no hand can paint! The bitterness in his cup of sorrow, as a sufferer bearing imputed sin, no tongue can tell! We can only say, and rejoice that heaven bids us say it, that this is the divine plan of redeeming love, to put another in our room, and that other one the Father's own beloved Son, to obey for us the law, and exhaust for us the curse! It is done! It is finished! What a shout of victory! What tidings of great joy for a lost world! What fulness of salvation must be here!

The plan was Heaven-appointed!

The Saviour is the Eternal Son!

The very place he takes is ours!

The work he undertakes to do, and the suffering he consents to bear, are the work and suffering which alone provide for us a righteousness in which to appear before the Holy God. It is done! It is finished!

Then, glorious conclusion for me, a sinner, I may be saved, and saved at once! Saved through the faith which reckons that it is *Christ for me! Christ for me!*

Oh, how a word like this strikes at the root of all self-righteousness, and all man's fancied ways of getting mercy of the Lord! And how it opens up before the anxious trembling soul a path of light and life, which otherwise would be closed and dark!

1. Speak not of any other way of life than this; for had there been a possibility of any, would Jesus have ever died? Would the Father have ever given up his Son to agonise and bleed for men? The cross, the cross, and the cry, 'It is finished!' give a deathblow to all self-righteousness!

2. But speak not of holding back from that cross now, and refusing to venture near thy God, because of thy felt unworthiness and sin! Come, rather, near. It is an accomplished work for you. Redemption is finished. Salvation secured. God's righteousness brought in and nigh; and at the cross of Jesus life and heaven for you for the taking, for the receiving, as a poor lost sinner who consents to be for ever a debtor to divine grace, and saved by the blood of the slain Lamb of God!

It is finished! God is satisfied; are you? Only believe and live!

III. I take yet another bearing of the word—namely, on *the final accomplishment of redemption work secured*. 'It is finished!' In telling from that cross of the past, this cry is for the far future.

For that cross of Jesus, the central point in redemption work, is the centre of this world's history, the centre of the purposes of God bearing on eternity. It tells of the final restitution of all things. It tells in anticipation of that other final cry 'It is done,' for that cross accomplishes all, secures all. On the ground of that atoning work shall a 'multitude which no man can number' be saved out of a lost world, and the world itself recovered, regained for God.

It matters not how long, even since the days of Calvary, the clouds over earth are dark, the day of glory *shall* appear in all its brightness!

It matters not how long the enemy seems to triumph, and how unlikely it appears that the kingdom of righteousness and peace shall fill the earth. The cross has secured it all!

What wonders have been wrought already since that dark day of Calvary! What a power has issued from that loud cry, 'It is finished!'

How many souls has this word attracted! How many sinking hearts has it comforted! What a change on the face of lands and nations even, from that gospel of Jesus, which no civilisation could accomplish!

What a change for eternity on the hopes and destinies of millions! And what wonders shall yet be wrought! 'I, if I be lifted up, from the earth, will draw all men unto me' (John 12:32).

Do you despair of the church and the world? Remember the loud cry of Calvary, 'It is finished!'

Do you tremble in view of the power of the forces which oppose the cause and kingdom of the Messiah? Remember, 'It is finished!'

To the grand consummation of the revealed glory of redemption work, of the Saviour and the saved, all things tend; and if you ask for that which sealed their destiny, and secured the world for God and God's Anointed, I point to the tree of Calvary, and that loud cry, 'It is finished!' from the dying Son of God.

I have but indicated as suggestive of precious, solemn thoughts, some of the bearings of this great word, of this loud cry. He that hath an ear let him hear this, 'It is finished!'

Should not this dying word of the Saviour reach every heart and affect every soul of man? Who ought to have so great an interest in Calvary as the sinners for whom Jesus died?

Is *sin*, as God knows it, an evil of unspeakable magnitude?

Is *salvation* a blessing whose value we shall fail fully to estimate even in the ages of eternity?

And does the cry, 'It is finished!' tell of sin put away, and salvation brought nigh? Does it tell of barriers broken down which no sinner could ever pass, and a righteousness brought in which is the very righteousness of God?

Does it tell of justice satisfied, and the law kept, and God honoured, and that nothing now remains but that this salvation be accepted?

Then, what glad tidings are these for the lost, what a jubilee sound is that great loud cry, 'It is finished!'

I know that even *it* falls on the *ear only* of a careless world, for if men feel not that they are lost, they cannot care for a Saviour. And what a picture have you of a lost world in the busy bustling scenes of this world's pleasures, in which men are unmoved by the tidings of the cross, untouched by the cry of salvation secured for man!

But has God awakened you by his Spirit, have you felt the vanity of earth without *him*? Has your burdened soul sought rest, and your empty heart sighed for God to fill it? Did you come in anxiety of soul and search about for salvation somewhere? Did you spend your days in looking for something in your heart to make you think that God would receive you? Did you strive to get some preparation ere you could venture nigh to the cross? And did you find it all to be vain and fruitless effort? Ah, say if peace came not in, and the burden fell not from your heart, when, taught of heaven, you grasped the truth involved in this great word, 'It is finished!'

Thus would I make application of the word, 'It is finished!' *Jesus* has said it. Have *you*?

'It is finished!' It is true of *his* great work of redemption for sinners, of salvation secured for the lost!

'It is finished!' Is it true of *your* reception of him? Is that work over and past? Have you believed on the Son of God?

How apt we are to leave this an uncertain matter, to delay coming to a sure conclusion, to imagine that there is a kind of virtue in doubt and hesitation!

If thou *art* to try and prepare a salvation for thy soul, or make thy soul worthy of the salvation of God, if thou art to work out a righteousness for thyself, it *will* take time, it will take eternity, and eternity will not do it! But if it is all secured, accomplished, finished, offered, pressed upon thee, as God's gift of love, what hinders? Only this, 'Ye will not come to me that ye might have life' (John 5:40).

My fellow-sinner, are you *unsaved*, and are you *careless* and unconcerned?

Would that God would awaken you as you read these pages! Would that he would awaken you on earth! On earth—where there is a Saviour's love and a free salvation, and the gospel sounding liberty and life. It is worthwhile your pausing, pausing here, and now, to let that loud cry fall upon your ear—it may reach your heart today, 'It is finished!'

My fellow-sinner, are you *unsaved*, and are you *anxious*?

Then here, here at my Saviour's cross, here in the glorious truth of this great loud cry, 'It is finished!' is rest for your troubled soul. What more need you?

Atonement made! Righteousness brought in! Justice satisfied! God honoured! Jesus waiting to be gracious, and longing in his outstretched arms to welcome you! *Only believe and live.*

My fellow-sinner, are you *saved*?

Then try to enter more than ever into the joy and liberty of such a word as this, and as you stay your soul anew on Jesus and his finished work, try with glad heart to anticipate the day when you shall be able to say, 'I am now ready to be offered, and the time of my departure is at hand. I have fought a good fight, I have finished my course, I have kept the faith: Henceforth there is laid up for me a crown of right-eousness, which the Lord, the righteous Judge, shall give me at that day; and not to me only, but unto all them also that love his appearing' (2 Tim. 4:6-8).

Anticipate the day when the number of the saved shall be complete, and the kingdoms of the world shall be the Lord's, when this 'It is finished' of Calvary shall be caught up for the final shout of victory, 'It is done!' (Rev. 16:17).

VII

Father, into thy hands I commend my spirit.

For though the strife was sore,
Yet in His parting breath
Love masters agony, the soul that seemed
Forsaken, feels His present God again,
And in His Father's arms,
Contented, dies away.

VII

Father, into thy hands I commend my spirit.—LUKE 23:46.

WHAT a change from the darkness and desertion of the Redeemer's soul, into the dawning light of eternal day! Surely the bitterness of death is past! 'Father, into thy hands I commend my spirit: and having said thus, he gave up the ghost.'

May God unfold to our hearts the meaning, and the power, and the preciousness of this dying word of Jesus!

I. I note *the work* of the dying one; for we must apprehend the mystery of that death.

It is like no other death, this death of Jesus!

It stands out like his birth, miraculously alone! It is the 'Prince of life' dying! It is the incarnate Son of God giving up the ghost on a cross! It is a *sacrificial* death! Death! The very name is solemn, startling. Instinctively, the living shudder and shrink from it. Death! It tells of sin, and this is its sting!

Death coming into our world by sin! Death the wages of sin!

Oh, what a picture of desolation is our world as presenting a history of death! From Eden onwards to this hour. From that first home on to ours, the young, the strong, the fair have fallen in millions under that stern Reaper's scythe. 'The wages of sin is death' (Rom. 6:23).

One surely will be exempt from dying, the Lord, the 'Prince of life,' especially as he comes to abolish death, and destroy him that has the power of it. Nay, but he comes to die. Only see the '*death of death*' in the death of Christ. Taking imputed guilt, he takes it to bear it, and to bear it all away by paying the penalty—by dying.

'It is Christ that died!' as if none other died; for this is a sacrifice, Heaven's own great sacrifice, a redeeming death as the fruit of God's everlasting love to man.

Aye, and *his* is the death which destroys death, which makes the death of believers now but the shadow of dying, though it deepens the gloom of the second death of unbelievers.

This is the mystery of the death of Calvary. This is the work of the dying one.

II. I note the *attitude* of the dying one. His eye is towards his Father. 'Father, into thy hands I commend my spirit.'

1. Is he making satisfaction for sin on that cross? It is God who is the offended one! 'Against thee, thee only have I sinned.' It is to him the Saviour undertook to make full satisfaction for sin! Ah, now he is making 'his soul an offering for sin.' He is paying the price of our redemption into the hands

of God. *His* life for ours, *his* soul for ours. Must *we* die? He dies for us, for our sins, in our stead. The price is paid and put into the hands of God. The Son gives it, the Father takes it, all in fulfilment of the eternal counsels of redeeming love!

2. Another thought here on the attitude of Jesus. Alone with his Father.

It is one great thought of dying—*alone with God*. When King Hezekiah got the message, 'Thus saith the Lord, Set thine house in order; for thou shalt die, and not live,' we are told that 'he turned his face to the wall, and prayed unto the Lord' (2 Kings 20:1, 2). Away from men unto God, to God alone—to be alone with God. And the sight I get of Jesus dying is, alone with his Father.

I refer not so much to the circumstance that so many of the words from the cross were for others, his prayer for his murderers, his promise to the penitent thief, his consolation for his mother!

I refer not so much to the fact, that even the words for himself told so much of the depth of his suffering and sorrow, 'My God, my God, why hast thou forsaken me?' 'I thirst!'

I refer specially to the second last word, which we sometimes call the latest when we sing,

> 'Tis finished—was His latest voice.

That was his farewell to *earth*. It was a word for heaven, too, and hell, but it spake specially to earth the glad tidings of the gospel, and left the substance of the great message of peace for sinners, and told by anticipation of the grand accomplishment of the whole great scheme of redeeming love.

But now all is over! All things predicted of him in the Scriptures fulfilled!

All types and prophecies and promises accomplished! All his obedience and suffering past! All that was required for the great atonement over, save the fast approaching act of dying!

And now he is going home—home to his Father's bosom—home to his mediatorial crown—home for the eternal reward of dying love in the love everlasting of his own Father, and the crown of a ransomed world!

This absorbs his dying moments. This is his dying attitude, with his face towards his Father alone.

It reminds one of that other word which opens his great intercessory prayer, 'Father, the hour is come'; *the* hour, the one hour of time which Father and Son so well know, the one hour of time on which from eternal ages the thoughts of love have settled.

On the cross, as the curtain is falling, as his head is bowing that he may die, we hear, 'Father, into thy hands I commend my spirit.'

What an end to a life like his! What an end to the earthly course of mediatorial work, on which from eternity he and his Father have had their eye!

What a word I may say, in passing, for those who fall asleep in Jesus! What an attitude for their dying hour! What an end to their chequered life! What a consummation of their hopes begotten by redeeming love! What an entrance-word for them, as for their Saviour and forerunner, into untold glory!

III. I note *the Spirit* of the dying one.

1. And here you see the voluntary surrender of his life by the Son of God.

He dies as the 'Prince of life,' though it be on the accursed tree. 'No man taketh my life from me, but I lay it down of myself. I have power to lay it down, and I have power to take it again' (John 10:18). This voluntary surrender of himself is seen in his whole course of suffering down to the close, and you find that while afterwards the fact of Christ's death is spoken of under the expression 'He died,' the Evangelists never use this word in their narrative, but rather, 'He gave up the ghost.' He 'yielded up the ghost.'

True, he had given himself up as the obedient Son, to suffer and to die!

True, he had put himself under the law's curse, and in the hands of justice, as if *he* were the sinner, and 'the wages of sin is death.'

But yet, strange mingling of weakness and strength! Strange sight involved in the 'Prince of life' dying, in the Lord, who has 'the keys of death,' opening the door for himself! He does not die like one feeling the approach of death and bowing to it; but when he knew his work was over, when he scanned the Scriptures concerning himself and saw them all fulfilled, when his time was come, of his own accord he breathed out his soul; it was 'a determinate delivering up of his spirit to the Father.' 'Father, into thy hands I commend my spirit.'

2. What a picture, too, is here of obedient love, and holy peace, and calm confidence—'Father.'

It is the old word which has been his stay from the child-hood of his days on earth, as it had been his eternal word in the bosom of his Father !

It was the one word which came out from the deep silence of the thirty years, ere his public ministry began, 'Wist ye not that I must be about my Father's business?' (Luke 2:49).

Deserted by friends, 'enduring the contradiction of sinners against himself,' it was this that consoled his spirit, 'Yet I am not alone, for my Father is with me' (John 8:16).

Nailed to his cross, his *first* word on it and his *last* is 'Father.' 'Father, forgive them, for they know not what they do.' 'Father, into thy hands I commend my spirit.'

And all the more precious is this last word, this dying word of faith and peace and hope, after the deep gloom of soul, of which the darkness over nature was but the faintest type. Now 'the darkness is past, and the light shineth.'

What a contrast on that cross—the darkness and the light—bringing out for us the mingling of these two thoughts, the Sin-bearer, the forsaken one, and yet this one, the Father's own beloved, dying in light!

Strange combination! and yet just what is needed for our

salvation. Never darkness so deep, never light so bright, never a death so bitter, never an end so peaceful, never sin so concentrated and the curse so lying on any head as his, here alone the curse expended and sin taken away.

The Saviour's end is one of purest light, and his dying word one of deepest peace. It is like a great stream which has passed its winding course over rugged rocks, widening and deepening in the broad valley, and pouring its now peaceful waters into the vast ocean, 'Father, into thy hands I commend my spirit.'

IV. I note *our interest* in the death and dying word of Jesus.

Father—it is the name, the title which we have forfeited by sin.

It is the word he brings down from heaven to teach to prodigals here, that in his name and after him we may lisp it, 'Abba, Father.'

And see here, with himself, the Son puts into his Father's hand his church, his people, all of us who are bought with his blood and believe on his name!

Oh, precious thought, that as the gloom which rested on this forsaken one was our desert, the light which shines on the accepted Son and Saviour shines on us! As free now as he are we, as accepted *as* the beloved, because accepted *in* him, and now as it were already taken into the Father's presence, already presented there as a church redeemed, and washed and justified and sanctified in the name, and by the righteousness and blood, of the Son of God!

One with Jesus! this is the thought; a thought which tells out all salvation work.

One with Jesus! not only as he has us on his heart in his great prayer of intercession, and presents us to the Father thus, but one with him in all his work. Our nature his, we living in his earthly life, and dying on his bloody cross, and buried in his narrow tomb, and rising in his risen life, and sitting now in heavenly places with himself to appear with him when he comes as part of himself, 'His bride, the Lamb's wife.'

In the Father's hands with Jesus we are accepted now, and into the Father's hands committed now, to be delivered by Jesus along with the whole church when the end cometh, and the kingdom is delivered up to the Father, and God is all in all. 'Father, into thy hands I commend my spirit.'

Was there ever a deathbed like that of the Son of God?

Ever one so compassed with dark and bitter sorrow, as earth and hell combined their malignant cruelty?

Ever one from which there issued such instructions for the world, not only in words which preach the gospel to the living, but in comfortable words for the dying?

Ever one whose issue was so bright and calm out from the deep gloom of a forsaken one into the peaceful 'Father, into thy hands I commend my spirit?'

It gives us a twofold lesson for dying and living, for death and life.

1. For dying.

Our safety, if we are simple believers in Jesus; for our spirits are committed to the Father already in that very dying word of our Saviour, and if that prayer was heard, and he was accepted, so are we.

It matters not where we die, or when; and if believers in Jesus, in one sense it matters not how we die. It may be in the calm peace of a quiet sea, or with the fresh breeze from heaven of triumphant joy, that you enter the haven; or it may be a stormy end to a tempestuous voyage; it may be in darkness or in light; but if you are Christ's you are safe, and the word which heaven utters over your grave is, 'Asleep in Jesus,' 'So giveth he his beloved sleep.'

But what a lesson is here for our dying hour, *how* to die! With Scripture on his lips, Jesus died. It is a word from that psalm of faith, the Thirty-first, 'Into thy hands I do commit my spirit.' In the human way of faith he walked, and on the Scripture, which was his guide in life, he stayed his soul in death.

Let that same word of God be our stay and strength in life, in death, in sunshine and in cloud, in joy and in sorrow, so shall we be followers of Jesus.

And, precious thought! *I* may take, when dying, *his* dying word, and through the now open way, use it as the martyr Stephen did when, committing himself to the Father through the Son, he cried to him whom he saw standing on the right hand of God, 'Lord Jesus, receive my spirit' (Acts 7:59).

2. For life.

It was after the cry, 'It is finished!' that there came the last peaceful word, 'Father, into thy hands I commend my spirit.'

He had his work to do, and he did it. His work of holy obedience, 'to bring in' for us an 'everlasting righteousness.' His work of atonement to make an end of sin; and not till all was accomplished did he breathe out his soul.

As with Jesus so must it be with us.

We have our work to do, and our cry to utter, 'It is finished!' telling of our acceptance for our soul's life of the finished work of Jesus.

And this first work done, we have a life to live of holy obedience, of earnest hearty work for God, for the salvation of our fellow men, for the advancement of his glory and kingdom.

Oh, that ours may be a life which shall have a peaceful end! a life not wholly lost, a life rather filled up with work for our loving Lord, that able to say, 'I have fought a good fight, I have finished my course, I have kept the faith' (2 Tim. 4:7), we may breathe our spirit calmly away into the Father's hands in the language of the dying word of Jesus, or of the old psalm, which suits a sinner well, 'Into thine hand I commit my spirit; thou hast redeemed me, O Lord God of truth' (Psa. 31:5).

'So shall we ever be with the Lord.'

HEARKEN! The voice of the Lord!
And hearken yet again.
Hearken! The *silence* of the Lord!
The broken voice, which pled with many tears,
Is hushed, is done with fears and tremblings now;
The seal of death is pressed upon the mouth
Which spake as never any man did speak.
Hearken! The silence of the Lord!
This silence speaketh with a thunder-voice.
He sleepeth in His bloody, borrowed tomb,
In darkness and in silence, with the dead.
O pierced hands! that were stretched out in vain
All day to man, and stretched out at last—
But not in vain—for man upon the tree,
At rest at last. O weary, wounded head!
Marked with the crown! He said He had no place
To lay His head, but He hath found a place.
O feet! that hath been weary with the hills
Of Ephraim and Judah—going oft
By stony mountain-tracks to seek His sheep,
The lost sheep, scattered on the burning hills
Of Israel—at rest, at rest, at last!
Hearken! The silence of the Lord!
For God hath given His Beloved sleep—
He takes His sabbath-rest, for all His work is done.
Hearken! The silence of the Lord!